Study Guide of Simple Lithuanian Phrases
Adventures in the Park with Marcijona:
The Red Squirrel

Grayce Lynn Lily

Introduction

Study Guide of Simple Lithuanian Phrases Adventures in the Park with Marcijona is a companion to the *Adventures in the Park with Marcijona: the Red Squirrel* book. The book is a children's pictorial and text story about the daily life of Marcijona, a red squirrel that lives in Vilnius, Lithuania. Marcijona the red squirrel is a member of an endangered species.

The *Adventures in the Park with Marcijona* book does not use the Lithuanian language. It merely lists simple Lithuanian and English phrases to introduce a language used by a different culture. It was felt that using the English and Lithuanian in the text of the story would be too distracting.

Pictures from the book are used to show examples of combined vocabulary words. This is not a travel vocabulary learning tool. It is for entertaining children while giving them some simple language skills from another culture. The words identified by number on page 5 are also given in the examples. Example: Hello, my name is Marcijona. #3,7, and 1. Labas! Mano vardas Marcijona.

How to use this Guide

On the following pages you will find the phrase list of Lithuanian/English words along with examples where they could be used. There are many translation/pronunciation sites online, if one desires to learn more.

There is historical information about the red squirrel and an old woodcutting from the 1600's. Children familiar with digital cameras in this day-and-age, will need to have this old artisan craft explained to them.

Woodcarving was a method of communicating and preserving history. A teaching moment, perhaps someone in the family does woodworking, building furniture, or other hand crafts that the children can relate to.

The book begins with Marcijona greeting the children by stating her name and where her home is: a park in Vilnius, Lithuania.

Following that is a bonus map of the Old Town of Vilnius. This ancient map of Vilnius (1576), shows a historical view to the child, which can be used as a stepping-stone for further study of the history of Lithuania if so desired.

Modern day Vilnius is shown, as the watercolors used in the story are from the present day. An informational and historical review on Vilnius and the Old Town are included.

A color wheel showing colors mentioned and highlighted in the story has been provided to enable color recognition.

Some Lithuanian Phrases

Lithuanian   **English**

1. Marcijona .... Marci
2. Lietuviu .... Lithuania
3. labas .... hello
4. viso .... bye
5. voverė .... squirrel
6. taip .... yes
7. mano vardas .... my name is
8. prašau .... please
9. ačiū .... thank you
10. iki .... see you
11. raudona voverė .... red squirrel
12. kekstas .... jay
13. ne .... no
14. prašom .... you're welcome

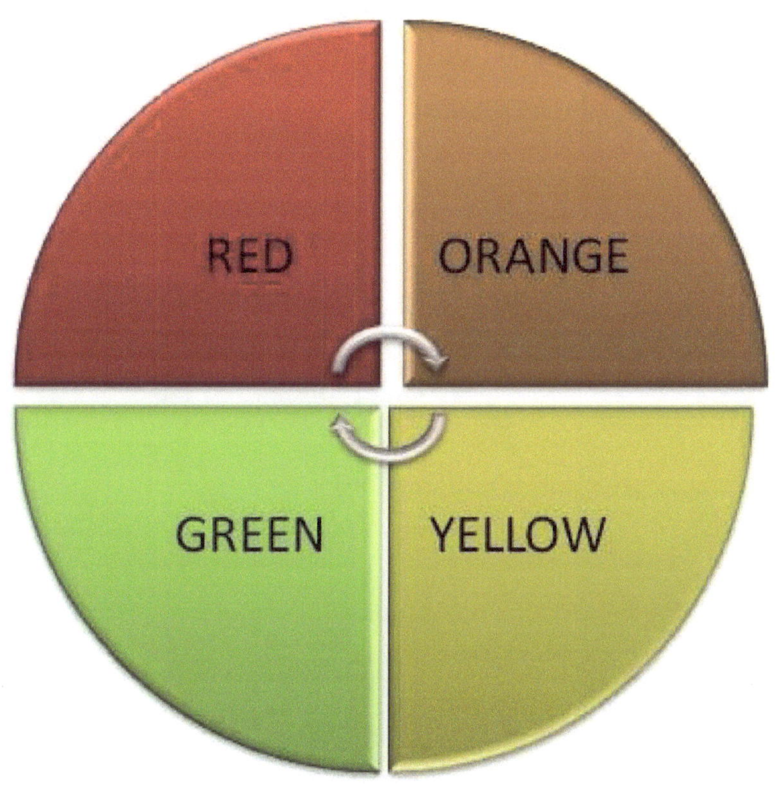

Identifying colors that are shown in the book.

The Red Squirrel

The European red squirrel is protected in most of Europe, as it is an endangered species.

The red squirrel first appeared 10,000 years ago, at the end of the last Ice Age, when the land between Britain and Europe began to disappear.

The photos of the red squirrels depicted in these oil and watercolor renderings were photographed in Vilnius, Lithuania.

Écureuil commun d'Europe (Sciurus vulgaris).

A woodcutting from the 1600's

Labas! Hi!
Mano vardas, Marcijona.   My name is Marcijona.
phrases #3, 7, 1.

Vilnius, Lietuviu, 1576. ne no/not A bonus, ne in the book. Use this map as a way to introduce more studies of Lietuviu.   phrases #2, 13.

Lietuviu. Vilnius, Lithuania   taip   yes
Ex: Is this the Vilnius, Lietuviu of today?
Taip. it is.   phrases #2, 6.

My home is a green park in Vilnius.

prašau   please
phrase #8 could have been used here.
Prašau follow me.
I'd like to show you my home.

red and green

red, green, yellow, and orange

voverė squirrel
phrase #5

raudona voverė   red squirrel
pictured throughout the book
phrase #11

A raudona voverė in winter.
It has more and darker fur to keep warm .
phrase #11.

ačiū   thank you   **Ačiū** for sharing the
food with me.   phrase #9.

kekstas   jay   prašom   you're welcome
phrases #12, 14.

viso   bye   iki   see you   phrase #4,9.

viso   bye   **ačiū**   thank you   iki   see you
Viso **ačiū** for coming, iki soon.
phrases #4, 9 and 10.

Fun Facts

Red squirrels do not hibernate in winter, they just slow down when winter comes.

They live high up in trees in nests called a drey made from twigs, leaves and moss.

They can jump more than 13 feet, they are good swimmers too.

They can hang upside down.

Written by and watercolor renditions
Grayce Lynn Lily

City of Vilnius

Vilnius is the capital of Lithuania and its largest city,with a population of a little over a half million people. Vilnius is in the southeast part of Lithuania and is the second largest city in the Baltic States.

Vilnius is the seat of the main government institutions of Lithuania and the Vilnius District Municipality. Vilnius is known for the architecture in its Old Town.

Vilnius was declared a UNESCO World Heritage Site in 1994. This means that it is legally protected by international treaties and judged important to the collective interests of humanity.

The Old Town of Vilnius, one of the largest surviving medieval old towns in Northern Europe, has an area of 3.59 square kilometers (887 acres).

It encompasses 74 quarters, with 70 streets and lanes numbering 1,487 buildings with a total floor area of 1,497,000 square meters.

Examples of some of Europe's greatest architectural styles – Gothic, Renaissance, Baroque and Neoclassical are found here.

Historic Gediminas Castle Tower, Old Town, Vilnius.

You have come to the end of our visit to ***Study Guide of Simple Lithuanian Phrases Adventures in the Park with Marcijona: The Red Squirrel***, a vocabulary and study book.

The pictorial and text story ***Adventures in the Park with Marcijona: The Red Squirrel***, is about the daily life of Marcijona, a red squirrel that lives in Vilnius, Lithuania.

The book is available on Kindle and in print form. This companion ***Study Guide of Simple Lithuanian Phrases Adventures in the Park with Maracijjona: The Red Squirrel,*** is meant to help the children better understand cultures, other languages and history of the world they live in.

We have more adventures in Vilnius and Lithuania for us to go on, so look for me in other books soon.